Comets

Contents

Comets

by David Orme

Ransom

Trailblazers

Comets
by David Orme
Educational consultant: Helen Bird

Illustrated by Martin Bolchover and Cyber Media (India) Ltd.

Published by Ransom Publishing Ltd.
Radley House, 8 St. Cross Road, Winchester, Hampshire, SO23 9HX, UK
www.ransom.co.uk

ISBN   978 184167 424 7
First published in 2006
Reprinted 2007, 2011

Comets

Get
the
facts

Asteroids and meteorites

The solar system is
made up of the Sun
and the planets.

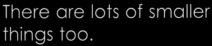

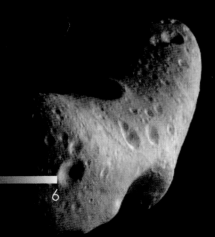

There are lots of smaller
things too.

Asteroids are like very small
planets. They go around the
Sun.

Meteorites are much smaller. They are made of rock or iron.

Most meteorites burn up in the air when they get to the Earth.

Sometimes they reach the ground.

Could a meteorite hit your house?

Yes! **In 1911 a dog was killed by a meteorite.**

In 1992 a meteorite made a hole in someone's car.

Comets

Comets are bigger than meteorites.

They come from far out
in the solar system.

They travel
around the Sun.

Comets are made
of ice and dust.

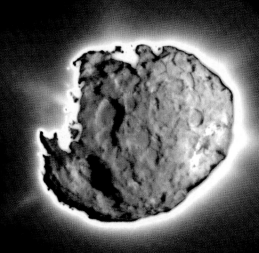

Sometimes they have a
bright tail.

Some comets can be seen
when they pass near the Sun.
Halley's comet comes close to
the Earth every 76 years.

In 1997 a new, bright comet was seen from the Earth. It was called comet Hale Bopp.

Some people think comets are signs that something bad is going to happen. There was a comet just before the great plague and fire of London.

A meteorite from Mars

When a comet or an asteroid hits a planet, bits of the planet can break off.

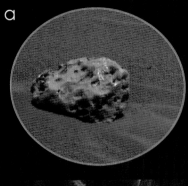

These bits go into space.

They can land on the Earth as meteorites.

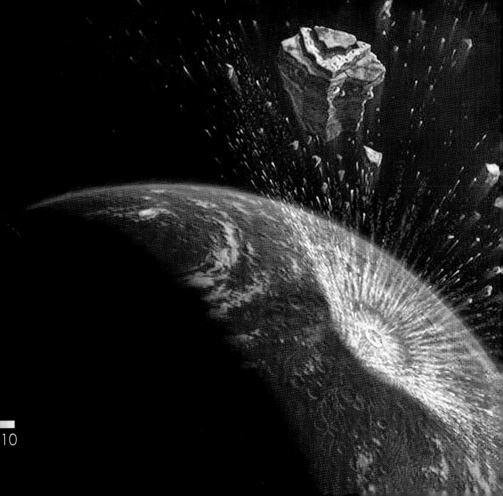

This meteorite came from the planet Mars.

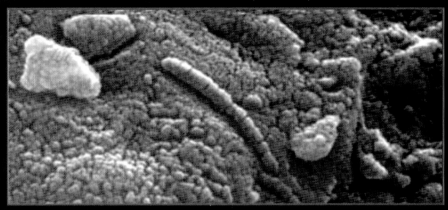

Look at the picture. What can you see?

Scientists think there is a fossil in the rock. They say it is the fossil of something that lived on Mars.

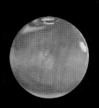

Space probes like this are looking for life on Mars.

Do you think they will find it?

The end of the dinosaurs?

65 million years ago, all the dinosaurs died.

Scientists think a comet or asteroid hit the Earth.

They have found a giant crater just here.

Gulf of Mexico

Chicxulub crater

Yucatan

Mexico

How could a comet or asteroid kill the dinosaurs?

Clouds of dust filled the sky.

No plants could grow.

Burning rocks started fires.

The water was poisoned.

A comet could hit the Earth again.

13

What are the dangers?

Meteorites reach the Earth
all the time.

They usually land where there
are no people, or in the sea.

No person has been killed
by one for a long time.

If a big comet or asteroid hits the
earth, human life could end.

If it hit the land there would be fire, and clouds of dust.

If it hit the sea it would make a big wave called a tsunami.

How big would it have to be to destroy all life?
- about 1 kilometre across.

There are thousands of asteroids and comets this big in space.

What can we do?

We can look out for asteroids and comets coming this way.

Then we can push them off course.

How can we do this?

We could land a rocket on the asteroid.

We could use its engine to push the asteroid off course.

We could make an explosion near the asteroid to push it off course.

We could blow up the asteroid into small pieces.

We would use a nuclear bomb to make the explosion.

Sounds like a good idea!

Yes, but there are problems.

We may not see the asteroid soon enough.

If things went wrong the asteroid could be pushed towards the Earth.

What do you think we should do?

Doom
from
Space

Chapter 1:
Earth is doomed!

All over the world, astronomers were checking their numbers. The world's best computers were on the case.

Out in the streets, people stared up into space. All they could see was a small, fuzzy shape with a faint tail. It didn't look dangerous.

There had been comets before. But this one was different. It was heading towards Earth. Unless something was done, the Earth was DOOMED.

The comet was about three miles across. At first, people thought that it wouldn't matter. It might fall in the sea, or in a desert. But scientists told them about the last big comet, sixty-five million years ago.

"It wiped out the dinosaurs. It wasn't hitting the Earth that did the damage, it was the dust."

Chapter 2:
A ten year winter

"The air will fill up with dust. Sunlight won't be able to get through. Crops will fail. And this could go on for ten years or more."

"There is only one chance of saving the world, but even that may not work. If we go for it, we will need to get ready now."

At Cape Canaveral Space Centre in Florida, the rocket was ready. On top of it was a nuclear bomb, the biggest ever made.

The plan was to explode the bomb near the comet. The explosion would push it off course. Scientists hoped it would be just enough to make the comet miss the Earth.

There had only been time to make one bomb. There was only one chance.

Chapter 3:
Lift off

"Five. Four. Three. Two. One. We have lift off! This mission will save the world."

The rocket blasted upwards. Everyone held their breath. If things went wrong, the bomb could go off and destroy everything for miles around.

But everything worked well. The rocket was soon in orbit around the Earth. The systems were checked. Everything was O.K. Now for the comet!

The great engines fired again. Slowly, the great rocket moved out of Earth orbit. The comet was ten million miles away, but getting closer to Earth every minute.

Back on Earth, scientists were checking the numbers again. And they found something surprising.

The comet had changed course!

"It's not going to hit the Earth after all. Stop the rocket!"

But it was too late.

Chapter 4:
A huge explosion

Scientists tried to change the rocket's course, but its radio had stopped working. On and on it went. At last it reached the comet.

It was meant to explode near the comet, to push it off course. But the comet had moved. The rocket hit it full on. There was a huge explosion. Even people on Earth could see the great flash in the sky.

"At least that's got rid of the comet," people said. "We'll be safe now."

But they were wrong.

The explosion had blown the comet to bits and blasted them towards Earth. Instead of one comet, there were now hundreds of bits of radioactive rock heading for the Earth.

People once again stood out in the streets and looked up into space.

Were they doomed after all?

Comets word check

asteroid	kilometre
astronomers	lift off
blasted	Mars
bright	meteorite
Cape Canaveral	mission
comet	nuclear bomb
computers	planets
crater	poisoned
crops	radioactive
dangerous	rocket
dinosaurs	scientists
doomed	solar system
engine	space probes
explode	sunlight
explosion	surprising
Florida	systems
fossil	tsunami
fuzzy	usually